2021

Is Going to be the Best Year Ever!

Day Planner & Journal

2021 Is Going to be the Best Year Ever!

Day Planner & Journal

Serena Cassidy

Published by Lulu

Lulu.com

Morrisville, North Carolina

USA

Front cover: Branch silhouette illustration, Stock photos

First Edition 2020

Manufactured in the United States of America

Keywords: day planner, journal, diary, self-reflection, calendar, goal setting, Nova Scotia

ISBN 9781716633683

IF LOST, PLEASE RETURN TO:

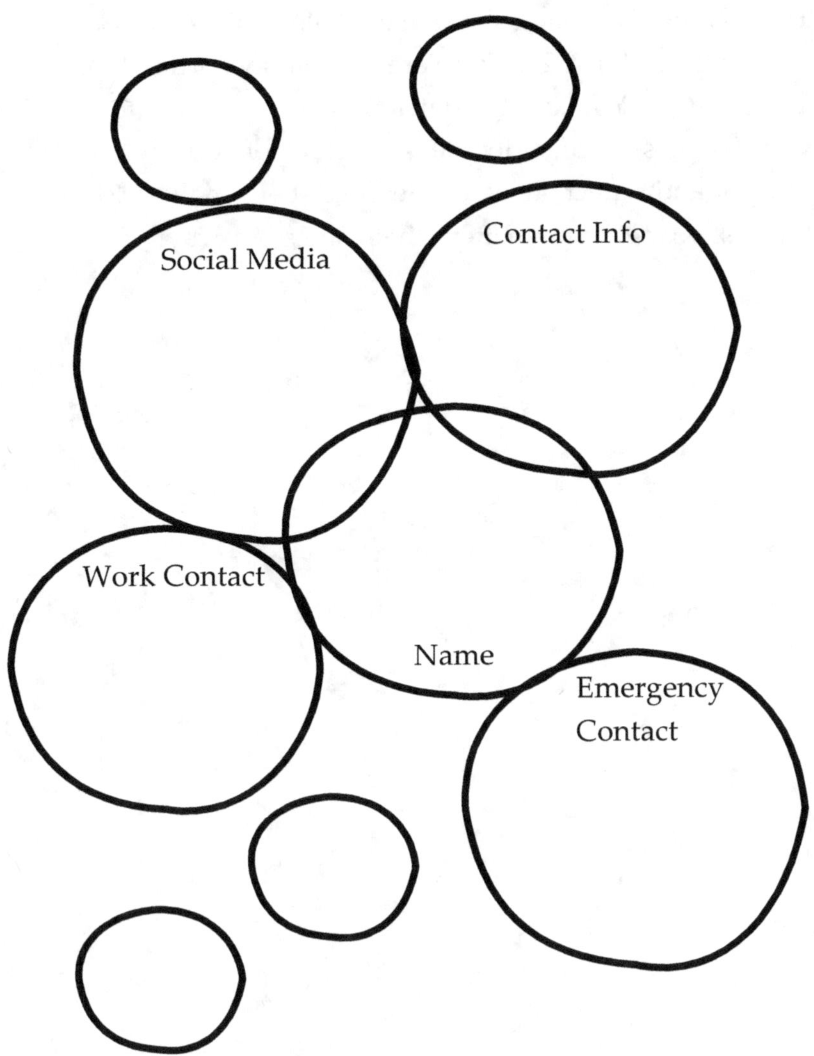

About this Planner

This planner is a blank slate to set goals and keep track
of your plans for 2021. There are no holidays printed in
this calendar. You add the dates that are important to
you. There is space to doodle, keep track of your
budget, and reflect on lessons learned. Let's make 2021
the best year ever no matter what comes our way!

2021 Calendar

JANUARY

S	M	T	W	T	F	S
					1	2
3	4	5	6	7	8	9
10	11	12	13	14	15	16
17	18	19	20	21	22	23
24	25	26	27	28	29	30
31						

FEBRUARY

S	M	T	W	T	F	S
	1	2	3	4	5	6
7	8	9	10	11	12	13
14	15	16	17	18	19	20
21	22	23	24	25	26	27
28						

MARCH

S	M	T	W	T	F	S
	1	2	3	4	5	6
7	8	9	10	11	12	13
14	15	16	17	18	19	20
21	22	23	24	25	26	27
28	29	30	31			

APRIL

S	M	T	W	T	F	S
				1	2	3
4	5	6	7	8	9	10
11	12	13	14	15	16	17
18	19	20	21	22	23	24
25	26	27	28	29	30	

MAY

S	M	T	W	T	F	S
						1
2	3	4	5	6	7	8
9	10	11	12	13	14	15
16	17	18	19	20	21	22
23	24	25	26	27	28	29
30	31					

JUNE

S	M	T	W	T	F	S
		1	2	3	4	5
6	7	8	9	10	11	12
13	14	15	16	17	18	19
20	21	22	23	24	25	26
27	28	29	30			

JULY

S	M	T	W	T	F	S
				1	2	3
4	5	6	7	8	9	10
11	12	13	14	15	16	17
18	19	20	21	22	23	24
25	26	27	28	29	30	31

AUGUST

S	M	T	W	T	F	S
1	2	3	4	5	6	7
8	9	10	11	12	13	14
15	16	17	18	19	20	21
22	23	24	25	26	27	28
29	30	31				

	SEPTEMBER					
S	M	T	W	T	F	S
			1	2	3	4
5	6	7	8	9	10	11
12	13	14	15	16	17	18
19	20	21	22	23	24	25
26	27	28	29	30		

	OCTOBER					
S	M	T	W	T	F	S
					1	2
3	4	5	6	7	8	9
10	11	12	13	14	15	16
17	18	19	20	21	22	23
24	25	26	27	28	29	30
31						

	NOVEMBER					
S	M	T	W	T	F	S
	1	2	3	4	5	6
7	8	9	10	11	12	13
14	15	16	17	18	19	20
21	22	23	24	25	26	27
28	29	30				

	DECEMBER					
S	M	T	W	T	F	S
			1	2	3	4
5	6	7	8	9	10	11
12	13	14	15	16	17	18
19	20	21	22	23	24	25
26	27	28	29	30	31	

IMPORTANT DATES

JANUARY	FEBRUARY
MARCH	APRIL
MAY	JUNE
JULY	AUGUST
SEPTEMBER	OCTOBER
NOVEMBER	DECEMBER

2021 Goals

#1

☐

#2

☐

#3

☐

#4

☐

#5

☐

#6

☐

#7

☐

#8

☐

#9

☐

#10

☐

Savings Tracker

How much do you want to save this year? You can colour in the template the next page as you grow your savings.

Savings Goal: _______________________________

Start Date: _______________________________

____
 I'M MOTIVATED TO SAVE UP FOR:

____

Date Goal Achieved: _______________________

Savings Tracker

DEBT PAYMENT TRACKER

	Credit Cards	Car Loan	Personal Loan	Mortgage	Total
Jan					
Feb					
Mar					
Apr					
May					
Jun					
Jul					
Aug					
Sep					
Oct					
Nov					
Dec					

Debt repayment goal (date): _______________________

2021 IN PIXELS

There's so much going on in the world, and in our lives, that it can be easy to feel overwhelmed. You can use the mood tracker as a visual to keep track of your feelings. Assign your own colours to the legend below. There's a blank space for you to add to as well.

Legend:

	OVERALL, I FEEL...
	GRATEFUL/ CONTENT
	HAPPY
	ANGRY/IRRITABLE
	SAD
	STRESS/ANXIETY
	OPTIMISTIC
	TIRED

	J	F	M	A	M	J	J	A	S	O	N	D
1												
2												
3												
4												
5												
6												
7												
8												
9												

	J	F	M	A	M	J	J	A	S	O	N	D
10												
11												
12												
13												
14												
15												
16												
17												
18												
19												
20												
21												
22												
23												
24												
25												
26												
27												
28												
29												
30												
31												

Monthly totals:

	J	F	M	A	M	J	J	A	S	O	N	D
GRATEFUL/ CONTENT												
HAPPY												
ANGRY/ IRRITABLE												
SAD												
STRESS/ ANXIETY												
OPTIMISTIC												
TIRED												

Notes:

____

____

____

____

____

____

____

THESE ACTIVITIES BRING ME JOY

BOOKS I'VE READ:

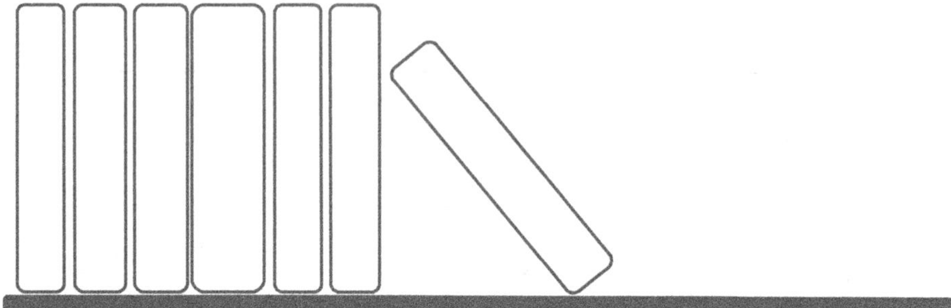

My Wishlist

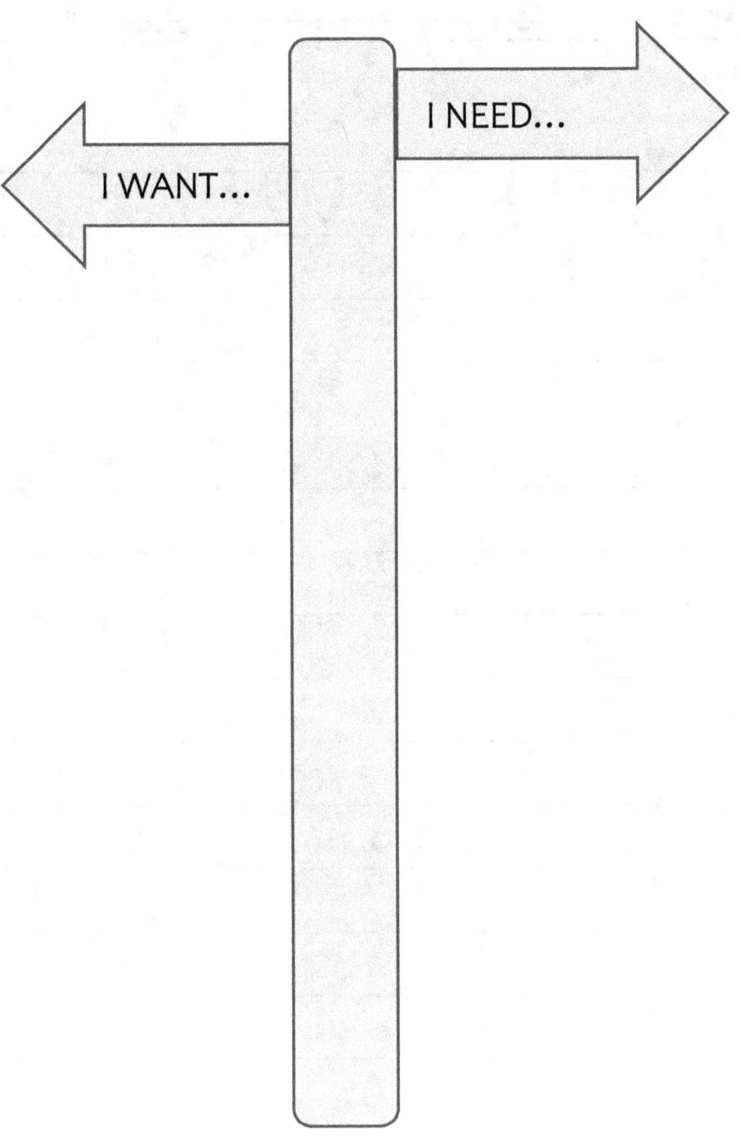

LESSONS LEARNED

TRAVEL – OH, THE PLACES I'VE BEEN....

DOODLE SPACE

JANUARY 2021

SUN	MON	TUE	WED	THU	FRI	SAT
					1	2
3	4	5	6	7	8	9
10	11	12	13	14	15	16
17	18	19	20	21	22	23
24	25	26	27	28	29	30
31						

Monthly Goals:

To Do:

Monthly Budget:

December 27 – January 2

Top three priorities:	To do list:

Weekly Budget $

27 | Sunday

28 | Monday

29 | Tuesday

30 | Wednesday

31 | Thursday

1 | Friday

2 | Saturday

January 3 – 9

Top three priorities:	To do list:

Weekly Budget $

3 | Sunday

4 | Monday

5 | Tuesday

6|Wednesday

7|Thursday

8|Friday

9|Saturday

January 10 – 16

Top three priorities:	To do list:

Weekly Budget $

10 | Sunday

11 | Monday

12 | Tuesday

13|Wednesday

14|Thursday

15|Friday

16|Saturday

January 17 – 23

Top three priorities:	To do list:

Weekly Budget $

17 | Sunday

18 | Monday

19 | Tuesday

20|Wednesday

21|Thursday

22|Friday

23|Saturday

<h1 style="text-align:center">January 24 – 30</h1>

Top three priorities:	To do list:

Weekly Budget $

24 Sunday

25 Monday

26 Tuesday

27|Wednesday

28|Thursday

29|Friday

30|Saturday

What went well this month?

____

____

____

____

What can I improve?

____

____

____

Notes:

____

____

____

DOODLE SPACE

FEBRUARY 2021

SUN	MON	TUES	WED	THUR	FRI	SAT
	1	2	3	4	5	6
7	8	9	10	11	12	13
14	15	16	17	18	19	20
21	22	23	24	25	26	27
28						

Monthly Goals:

To Do:

Monthly Budget:

January 31 - February 6

Top three priorities:	To do list:

Weekly Budget $

31 Sunday

1 Monday

2 Tuesday

3|Wednesday

4|Thursday

5|Friday

6|Saturday

February 7 – 13

Top three priorities:	To do list:

Weekly Budget $

7 | Sunday

8 | Monday

9 | Tuesday

10|Wednesday

11|Thursday

12|Friday

13|Saturday

February 14 – 20

Top three priorities:	To do list:

Weekly Budget $

14 | Sunday

15 | Monday

16 | Tuesday

17|Wednesday

18|Thursday

19|Friday

20|Saturday

February 21 – 27

Top three priorities:	To do list:

Weekly Budget $

21 | Sunday

22 | Monday

23 | Tuesday

24 | Wednesday

25 | Thursday

26 | Friday

27 | Saturday

What went well this month?

____

____

____

____

What can I improve?

____

____

____

____

Notes:

____

____

____

DOODLE SPACE

MARCH 2021

SUN	MON	TUE	WED	THU	FRI	SAT
	1	2	3	4	5	6
7	8	9	10	11	12	13
14	15	16	17	18	19	20
21	22	23	24	25	26	27
28	29	30	31			

Monthly Goals:

To Do:

Monthly Budget:

February 28 - March 6

Top three priorities:	To do list:

Weekly Budget $

28 | Sunday

1 | Monday

2 | Tuesday

3 | Wednesday

4 | Thursday

5 | Friday

6 | Saturday

March 7 – 13

Top three priorities:	To do list:

Weekly Budget $

7 | Sunday

8 | Monday

9 | Tuesday

10 | Wednesday

11 | Thursday

12 | Friday

13 | Saturday

March 14 – 20

Top three priorities:	To do list:

Weekly Budget $

14 | Sunday

15 | Monday

16 | Tuesday

17 | Wednesday

18 | Thursday

19 | Friday

20 | Saturday

March 21 – 27

Top three priorities:	To do list:

Weekly Budget $

21 | Sunday

22 | Monday

23 | Tuesday

24|Wednesday

25|Thursday

26|Friday

27|Saturday

What went well this month?

____

____

____

____

What can I improve?

____

____

____

____

Notes:

____

____

____

DOODLE SPACE

APRIL 2021

SUN	MON	TUE	WED	THU	FRI	SAT
				1	2	3
4	5	6	7	8	9	10
11	12	13	14	15	16	17
18	19	20	21	22	23	24
25	26	27	28	29	30	

Monthly Goals:

To Do:

Monthly Budget:

March 28 – April 3

Top three priorities:	To do list:

Weekly Budget $

28 | Sunday

29 | Monday

30 | Tuesday

31|Wednesday

___

1|Thursday

___

2|Friday

___

3|Saturday

April 4 – 10

Top three priorities:	To do list:

Weekly Budget $

4 | Sunday

5 | Monday

6 | Tuesday

7 | Wednesday

8 | Thursday

9 | Friday

10 | Saturday

April 11 – 17

Top three priorities:	To do list:

Weekly Budget $

11|Sunday

12|Monday

13|Tuesday

14|Wednesday

15|Thursday

16|Friday

17|Saturday

April 18 – 24

Top three priorities:	To do list:

Weekly Budget $

18 | Sunday

19 | Monday

20 | Tuesday

21|Wednesday

22|Thursday

23|Friday

24|Saturday

April 25 – May 1

Top three priorities:	To do list:

Weekly Budget $

25 | Sunday

26 | Monday

27 | Tuesday

28 | Wednesday

29 | Thursday

30 | Friday

1 | Saturday

What went well this month?

____

____

____

____

What can I improve?

____

____

____

____

Notes:

____

____

____

____

DOODLE SPACE

May 2021

SUN	MON	TUE	WED	THU	FRI	SAT
						1
2	3	4	5	6	7	8
9	10	11	12	13	14	15
16	17	18	19	20	21	22
23	24	25	26	27	28	29
30	31					

Monthly Goals:

To Do:

Monthly Budget:

May 2 – 8

Top three priorities:	To do list:

Weekly Budget $

2 | Sunday

3 | Monday

4 | Tuesday

5|Wednesday

6|Thursday

7|Friday

8|Saturday

May 9 – 15

Top three priorities:	To do list:

Weekly Budget $

9 | Sunday

10 | Monday

11 | Tuesday

12 | Wednesday

13 | Thursday

14 | Friday

15 | Saturday

May 16 – 22

Top three priorities:	To do list:

Weekly Budget $

16 | Sunday

17 | Monday

18 | Tuesday

19 | Wednesday

20 | Thursday

21 | Friday

22 | Saturday

May 23 – 29

Top three priorities:	To do list:

Weekly Budget $

23|Sunday

24|Monday

25|Tuesday

26|Wednesday

27|Thursday

28|Friday

29|Saturday

What went well this month?

What can I improve?

Notes:

DOODLE SPACE

June 2021

SUN	MON	TUE	WED	THU	FRI	SAT
		1	2	3	4	5
6	7	8	9	10	11	12
13	14	15	16	17	18	19
20	21	22	23	24	25	26
27	28	29	30			

Monthly Goals:

To Do:

Monthly Budget:

May 30 – June 5

Top three priorities:	To do list:

Weekly Budget $

30 | Sunday

31 | Monday

1 | Tuesday

2|Wednesday

3|Thursday

4|Friday

5|Saturday

June 6 – 12

Top three priorities:	To do list:

Weekly Budget $

6 | Sunday

7 | Monday

8 | Tuesday

9|Wednesday

10|Thursday

11|Friday

12|Saturday

June 13 – 19

Top three priorities:	To do list:

Weekly Budget $

13 | Sunday

14 | Monday

15 | Tuesday

16|Wednesday

17|Thursday

18|Friday

19|Saturday

June 20 – 26

Top three priorities:	To do list:

Weekly Budget $

20 | Sunday

21 | Monday

22 | Tuesday

23|Wednesday

24|Thursday

25|Friday

26|Saturday

What went well this month?

____

____

____

____

What can I improve?

____

____

____

Notes:

____

____

____

DOODLE SPACE

July 2021

SUN	MON	TUE	WED	THU	FRI	SAT
				1	2	3
4	5	6	7	8	9	10
11	12	13	14	15	16	17
18	19	20	21	22	23	24
25	26	27	28	29	30	31

Monthly Goals:

To Do:

Monthly Budget:

June 27 – July 3

Top three priorities:	To do list:

Weekly Budget $

27 | Sunday

28 | Monday

29 | Tuesday

30 | Wednesday

---

1 | Thursday

---

2 | Friday

---

3 | Saturday

July 4 – 10

Top three priorities:	To do list:

Weekly Budget $

4 Sunday

5 Monday

6 Tuesday

7 | Wednesday

8 | Thursday

9 | Friday

10 | Saturday

July 11 – 17

Top three priorities:	To do list:

Weekly Budget $

11|Sunday

12|Monday

13|Tuesday

14|Wednesday

15|Thursday

16|Friday

17|Saturday

July 18 – 24

Top three priorities:	To do list:

Weekly Budget $

18 | Sunday

19 | Monday

20 | Tuesday

21|Wednesday

22|Thursday

23|Friday

24|Saturday

July 25 – 31

Top three priorities:	To do list:

Weekly Budget $

25 | Sunday

26 | Monday

27 | Tuesday

28|Wednesday

29|Thursday

30|Friday

31|Saturday

What went well this month?

____

____

____

____

What can I improve?

____

____

____

Notes:

____

____

____

DOODLE SPACE

August 2021

SUN	MON	TUE	WED	THU	FRI	SAT
1	2	3	4	5	6	7
8	9	10	11	12	13	14
15	16	17	18	19	20	21
22	23	24	25	26	27	28
29	30	31				

Monthly Goals:

To Do:

Monthly Budget:

August 1 – 7

Top three priorities:	To do list:

Weekly Budget $

1| Sunday

2| Monday

3| Tuesday

4 | Wednesday

5 | Thursday

6 | Friday

7 | Saturday

August 8 – 14

Top three priorities:	To do list:

Weekly Budget $

8 | Sunday

9 | Monday

10 | Tuesday

11|Wednesday

12|Thursday

13|Friday

14|Saturday

August 15 – 21

Top three priorities:	To do list:

Weekly Budget $

15 | Sunday

16 | Monday

17 | Tuesday

18|Wednesday

19|Thursday

20|Friday

21|Saturday

August 22 – 28

Top three priorities:	To do list:

Weekly Budget $

22 | Sunday

23 | Monday

24 | Tuesday

25|Wednesday

26|Thursday

27|Friday

28|Saturday

What went well this month?

____

____

____

____

What can I improve?

____

____

____

____

Notes:

____

____

____

____

DOODLE SPACE

September 2021

SUN	MON	TUE	WED	THU	FRI	SAT
			1	2	3	4
5	6	7	8	9	10	11
12	13	14	15	16	17	18
19	20	21	22	23	24	25
26	27	28	29	30		

Monthly Goals:

To Do:

Monthly Budget:

August 29 – September 4

Top three priorities:	To do list:

Weekly Budget $

29 | Sunday

30 | Monday

31 | Tuesday

1 | Wednesday

2 | Thursday

3 | Friday

4 | Saturday

September 5 – 11

Top three priorities:	To do list:

Weekly Budget $

5|Sunday

6|Monday

7|Tuesday

8 | Wednesday

9 | Thursday

10 | Friday

11 | Saturday

September 12 – 18

Top three priorities:	To do list:

Weekly Budget $

12 | Sunday

13 | Monday

14 | Tuesday

15|Wednesday

16|Thursday

17|Friday

18|Saturday

September 19 – 25

Top three priorities:	To do list:

Weekly Budget $

19 | Sunday

20 | Monday

21 | Tuesday

22|Wednesday

23|Thursday

24|Friday

25|Saturday

What went well this month?

____

____

____

____

What can I improve?

____

____

____

____

Notes:

____

____

____

____

DOODLE SPACE

October 2021

SUN	MON	TUE	WED	THU	FRI	SAT
					1	2
3	4	5	6	7	8	9
10	11	12	13	14	15	16
17	18	19	20	21	22	23
24	25	26	27	28	29	30
31						

Monthly Goals:

To Do:

Monthly Budget:

September 26 – October 2

Top three priorities:	To do list:

Weekly Budget $

26 | Sunday

27 | Monday

28 | Tuesday

29 | Wednesday

30 | Thursday

1 | Friday

2 | Saturday

October 3 – 9

Top three priorities:	To do list:

Weekly Budget $

3 | Sunday

4 | Monday

5 | Tuesday

6|Wednesday

7|Thursday

8|Friday

9|Saturday

October 10 – 16

Top three priorities:	To do list:

Weekly Budget $

10 | Sunday

11 | Monday

12 | Tuesday

13|Wednesday

14|Thursday

15|Friday

16|Saturday

October 17 – 23

Top three priorities:	To do list:

Weekly Budget $

17 | Sunday

18 | Monday

19 | Tuesday

20|Wednesday

21|Thursday

22|Friday

23|Saturday

October 24 – 30

Top three priorities:	To do list:

Weekly Budget $

24 | Sunday

25 | Monday

26 | Tuesday

27|Wednesday

28|Thursday

29|Friday

30|Saturday

What went well this month?

____

____

____

____

What can I improve?

____

____

____

____

Notes:

____

____

____

____

DOODLE SPACE

November 2021

SUN	MON	TUE	WED	THU	FRI	SAT
	1	2	3	4	5	6
7	8	9	10	11	12	13
14	15	16	17	18	19	20
21	22	23	24	25	26	27
28	29	30				

Monthly Goals:

To Do:

Monthly Budget:

October 31 – November 6

Top three priorities:	To do list:

Weekly Budget $

31 | Sunday

1 | Monday

2 | Tuesday

3|Wednesday

4|Thursday

5|Friday

6|Saturday

November 7 – 13

Top three priorities:	To do list:

Weekly Budget $

7 | Sunday

8 | Monday

9 | Tuesday

10|Wednesday

11|Thursday

12|Friday

13|Saturday

November 14 – 20

Top three priorities:	To do list:

Weekly Budget $

14 | Sunday

15 | Monday

16 | Tuesday

17|Wednesday

18|Thursday

19|Friday

20|Saturday

November 21 – 27

Top three priorities:	To do list:

Weekly Budget $

21 Sunday

22 Monday

23 Tuesday

24 Wednesday

25 Thursday

26 Friday

27 Saturday

What went well this month?

What can I improve?

Notes:

DOODLE SPACE

December 2021

SUN	MON	TUE	WED	THU	FRI	SAT
			1	2	3	4
5	6	7	8	9	10	11
12	13	14	15	16	17	18
19	20	21	22	23	24	25
26	27	28	29	30	31	

Monthly Goals:

To Do:

Monthly Budget:

November 28 – December 4

Top three priorities:	To do list:

Weekly Budget $

28|Sunday

29|Monday

30|Tuesday

1 | Wednesday

2 | Thursday

3 | Friday

4 | Saturday

December 5 – 11

Top three priorities:	To do list:

Weekly Budget $

5 | Sunday

6 | Monday

7 | Tuesday

8 | Wednesday

9 | Thursday

10 | Friday

11 | Saturday

Top three priorities:	To do list:

Weekly Budget $

12 | Sunday

13 | Monday

14 | Tuesday

15|Wednesday

16|Thursday

17|Friday

18|Saturday

December 19 – 25

Top three priorities:	To do list:

Weekly Budget $

19 | Sunday

20 | Monday

21 | Tuesday

22|Wednesday

23|Thursday

24|Friday

25|Saturday

December 26 – January 1

Top three priorities:	To do list:

Weekly Budget $

26 | Sunday

27 | Monday

28 | Tuesday

29|Wednesday

30|Thursday

31|Friday

1|Saturday

What went well this month?

____

____

____

____

What can I improve?

____

____

____

____

Notes:

____

____

____

____

DOODLE SPACE

2021 Is Going to be the Best Year Ever!

Day Planner and Journal

9781716633683